# Wacky Weather

## By Margery Niblock

# Contents

**Celebration Press**
Pearson Learning Group

# What's the Forecast?

*Sunshine and clear skies.*
*Cloudy with a chance of showers.*
*Hazy, hot, and humid.*
*Sleet and freezing rain.*

These are some common weather predictions that you've probably heard if you listen to television or radio weather reports.

Here are some predictions you most likely have not heard in a weather forecast:

*There will be no summer this year. Keep your shovel and your mittens handy.*

*Rain this afternoon, with a probability of falling frogs and fish, followed by grapefruit-size hail in the evening. Clearing Sunday morning, with winds at 231 miles per hour.*

Believe it or not, wacky weather like this has actually occurred—though not all at once!

# The Year Without a Summer

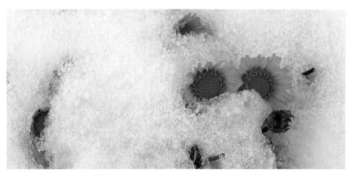

Have you ever seen snow in June?

Imagine waking up in mid-June and looking out the window to see the flowers and trees covered with snow. You would have to dress in your winter clothing. Shorts and T-shirts wouldn't keep you warm enough in that kind of weather!

Strange weather like this did happen during the summer of 1816 in much of Europe and the northern part of the United States. That's the reason 1816 is sometimes referred to as "the year without a summer."

Snow and frost in June, July, and August destroyed crops in New England and in most of Europe. That caused severe food shortages for people and farm animals. Practically all the corn crops were ruined.

People went hungry. Soup kitchens opened to feed them, but many people around the world still died from starvation. Because of the crop failures, many farm families from New England moved west toward the frontier that year.

On June 5, 1816, it was 83 degrees in Williamstown, Massachusetts, at noon. By the next day the highest temperature was only 45 degrees. One man wrote in his diary that "clothes that had been spread on the ground [to dry] the night before . . . were frozen stiff as in winter." On June 7 he wore "thick woolen clothes" and an overcoat. It was so cold that he also had to wear mittens.

The eruption of Mount Tambora in 1815 was the largest in recorded history.

## Mount Tambora Blows Its Top

This strange, cold weather was caused by a volcanic event on the other side of the world beginning April 5, 1815, and lasting about five days. Here is an explanation of what happened.

Pressure may build up inside a volcano from gases or lava. If this pressure is released suddenly, it can cause an explosion called an eruption. The eruption of Mount Tambora was the largest in recorded history.

The eruption of Mount Tambora on Sumbawa in Indonesia
had far-reaching effects.

Tambora is a **stratovolcano** located on
the island of Sumbawa in Indonesia.
Stratovolcanoes are cone-shaped. They
usually have steep sides made of layers
of cinders, ash, and hardened lava.

Tambora's eruption in 1815 hurled
millions of tons of ash, poisonous gas,
and solid fragments from the volcano
into the sky. About 10,000 people were
killed outright from the eruption.

## Look at That Sky!

The mixture of ash, gas, and solid particles traveled into the stratosphere, the area about 7 to 30 miles above the earth. There it formed a gigantic cloud of volcanic dust and began to cool the earth. The dust cloud did so by blocking sunlight as it moved around the earth. Enough sunlight was lost in some places to make temperatures drop more than 30° F. The cooling effect began in New England about 11 months after the eruption. The effects lasted about three years, but the summer of 1816 was the worst.

The eruption of Tambora did, however, have one positive result. The dust in the sky worked like a big filter, causing brilliant purple and red sunsets. Many people believe that J.M.W. Turner, a British artist famous for his beautiful landscapes, was inspired by the spectacular sunsets caused by Tambora.

Other large eruptions have cooled the earth in the same way, although not to the extent that Tambora did. They are the following volcanoes:

▲ Krakatoa (1883, Indonesia)

▲ Mount St. Helens (1980, United States)

▲ El Chichón (1982, Mexico)

▲ Mount Pinatubo (1991, Philippines)

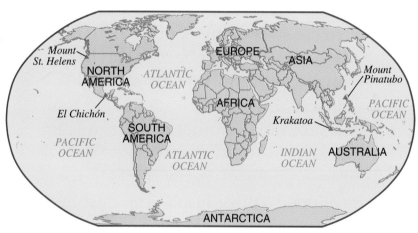

## Could It Happen Again?

Popocatépetl (often called Popo), is a beautiful snow-covered stratovolcano near Mexico City. Its name is an Aztec word meaning "smoking mountain."

After minor eruptions over some 500 years, Popo spewed out gases and ash in 1947 and again in 1994. Then it erupted violently in December 2000. About 50,000 people were moved away from the volcano to keep them safe as it spewed flaming rocks hundreds of feet into the sky.

We may not know the worldwide effects of this eruption for a long time. Compared with that of Tambora, this one was small. But if we experience some unusually cool weather, Popo may be the cause.

Popocatépetl erupted violently in December 2000.

# It's Raining Fish and Frogs!

During heavy downpours, people often complain that it's raining cats and dogs. That's just a saying, of course. Cats and dogs don't actually fall from the sky in a rainstorm.

Would it surprise you to hear a meteorologist predict rain containing frogs, toads, or fish? It has happened in many places, and the usual cause is a waterspout.

## Water Whirlwinds

Waterspouts are funnel-shaped, cloud-filled, spinning winds attached to the base of a cloud over water. They form over large bodies of water, such as oceans or lakes, when cool air high in the sky blows across warm water. They occur most often over warm ocean water.

A waterspout can reach forward speeds of about 80 miles per hour and may have winds spinning around inside the funnel at more than 60 miles per hour. It is like a small tornado, which is a whirling funnel of air attached to the base of a cloud over land.

This photo clearly shows the spinning column of clouds that forms a waterspout.

A waterspout may suck up water, along with the animals in it, and draw them into its **vortex**. That's a whirling mass of air or water that sucks objects near it toward its center.

In the Northern Hemisphere, winds in tornadoes and hurricanes whirl in a counterclockwise direction. In the Southern Hemisphere, the wind motions are reversed. This happens because the earth spins, which keeps the winds from blowing in a straight line. Winds in the Northern Hemisphere curve to their right. Winds in the Southern Hemisphere curve to their left.

A waterspout can carry water for miles. Eventually the water falls to the earth again as heavy rain. Frogs, toads, or fish may then fall from the sky! Reports of frogs and fish falling with rain have come from many areas, including Kansas, New York, and England.

A waterspout in Massachusetts in August of 1896 attracted a lot of attention because of its huge size. Thousands of people, including several scientists, saw it, and many people took photographs. Its height was estimated at over two thirds of a mile. At its base it was about 240 feet wide. Most waterspouts last only a few minutes, but this one lasted for about half an hour. Waterspouts can kill people and do great damage to small ships and boats.

Although waterspouts are seldom seen in the Western states, at least six were spotted on September 26, 1998, over Lake Tahoe, on the California-Nevada border. Residents photographed them from along the shore.

# Wind, Rain, Thunder, and Lightning

Hurricanes are tropical storms that contain rain, high wind, and usually thunder and lightning. When this type of storm occurs in the Atlantic or eastern Pacific ocean, it is called a hurricane. In the Philippines or in the China Sea, it is called a typhoon. It is called a cyclone in the Indian Ocean and around Australia. Huge masses of wind in hurricanes rotate around the eye, a calm center.

For a storm to be classified as a hurricane, it must have wind speeds of at least 74 miles per hour.

In the center of a hurricane is a calm, cloud-free zone called the eye.

Cyclones, hurricanes, and tornadoes do not form near the equator. Instead, a belt of calms, light winds, and sudden rains, called the doldrums, circles the oceans there. The doldrums are created when winds from both the north and the south meet at the equator and are forced upward. Before there were motor-powered ships, sailing ships used to get stuck in the doldrums. They would have to wait until there was enough wind to move again. People who are feeling gloomy may say they are "stuck in the doldrums."

The tremendous force of hurricane winds can move many things, including water. In October of 2000, Hurricane Keith emptied so much water from the Chetumal Bay off the coast of Belize that people were able to walk across the bay. Where do you think the water from the bay might have gone?

# Home of the World's Worst Weather

You may be surprised to learn that the home of some of the world's worst weather is in the United States on top of Mount Washington. This mountain is the highest peak in the northeastern United States. It is part of New Hampshire's White Mountains.

At 6,288 feet, Mount Washington isn't very tall, but its climate can be as harsh as Antarctica's. Many mountain climbers train on Mount Washington. The weather conditions are similar to those they would find on Mount Everest in the Himalayas.

The highest point on Earth, Mount Everest, is 29,035 feet high. The change in the official height from 29,028 feet to 29,035 feet was announced in November of 1999. The new height was measured with newly developed Global Positioning System satellite equipment.

Mount Washington has a combination of severe weather conditions—extreme cold, ice, and roaring winds. The average annual temperature at the top is only 26.5° F, and the weather is always unpredictable. On the morning of April 10, 1997, the thermometer read –8° F and later that day a wind gust of 108 mph was recorded!

### Where Am I?

Snowstorms sometimes occur on Mount Washington even in summer. Conditions may be so bad that visibility can plunge to zero. Forget mountain climbing. You could easily get lost in the parking lot!

Visibility can also be less than 50 feet in dense fog, and the summit is in fog 60 percent of the year. Sunshine is not a common sight. The fog and wind together cause huge buildups of frosty rime ice. Exposed objects look like frozen cakes with thick icing.

The severe weather on Mount Washington is a result of its location. The mountain sits right where three major storm tracks meet.

Scientists use the observatory on top of the mountain to conduct cold-weather experiments and to study climate. The Mount Washington Observatory transmits weather data to the National Weather Service many times a day.

Frosty rime ice covers buildings, posts, and other objects on Mount Washington in winter.

# Hold On!

Mount Washington may be the windiest place in the United States, perhaps even the world. It has hurricane-force winds about 100 days a year. Winds are clocked at over 100 miles per hour during every month of the year.

The highest wind speed that wasn't caused by a storm was measured on Mount Washington in April 1934. It was 231 miles per hour!

You can reach the top of Mount Washington by hiking, driving a car, or taking a cog railway train (a special train that goes up mountains). Whichever way you go, be prepared for the possibility of wacky weather.

The TV tower at the summit of Mount Washington was built to withstand winds of 300 miles per hour.

# Get Out the Hard Hats

On a hot summer afternoon, the sight of **cumulonimbus** clouds usually signals an approaching thunderstorm. These dark clouds, also called thunderheads, are often piled very high. If the proper conditions come together, the rainstorm they bring can turn into another form of wacky weather—an icy hailstorm.

**Hail** is small balls or lumps made up of layers of ice or snow. Strong upward movements of air in thunderstorms, called **updrafts**, form the hailstones. They start out as drops of water that are carried high up into the atmosphere.

Cumulonimbus clouds can bring thunderstorms and hail.

The droplets become cooled when they reach greater heights where the temperatures are below freezing. Then they freeze into solid pieces of ice. These little pieces of ice fall and then get tossed up again by the updrafts. As they are tossed up and down, more water droplets attach to them and freeze, making them larger. When they become heavy enough to overcome the force of the updrafts, they fall to the ground. Hail comes in different shapes and sizes.

| Sizes of Hail Compared to Everyday Items | | | |
|---|---|---|---|
| 1/4" | pea | 2" | hen egg |
| 1/2" | marble | 2 1/2" | tennis ball |
| 3/4" | penny | 2 3/4" | baseball |
| 1" | quarter | 3" | teacup |
| 1 1/4" | half dollar | 4" | grapefruit |
| 1 1/2" | walnut | 4 1/2" | soft ball |
| 1 3/4" | golf ball | | |

Meteorologists have made it easy for us to tell the different sizes of hailstones. They compare hail to the everyday items in this chart.

## Hail Alley

The high plains east of the Rocky Mountains have more hailstorms than any other area of the United States. This part of the country is called Hail Alley. Cheyenne, Wyoming, has an average of nine to ten hailstorms per season, more than any other American city.

Hailstones can cause great damage to crops, cars, rooftops, and animals. People can also be harmed or killed by hail, but most people usually find shelter during hailstorms.

If you slice through a hailstone, you will see that the ice forms in layers.

Large hailstones can reach speeds of over 100 miles per hour as they fall to the ground. The ice can build up and cause drifts like snowdrifts.

## One Scoop or Two?

Years ago, people would come outside after a storm, gather up the hailstones, and make ice cream! A June 1896 Kansas newspaper article told about a wagonload of hail that was "distributed among our people in town, who

This hailstone, which fell in Coffeyville, Kansas, is the largest ever recorded.

made ice cream with it. The hail was the size of walnuts when brought into town; they must have been as large as goose eggs when they dropped."

Although there have been reports of hailstones as large as an elephant, the largest hailstone confirmed by scientists landed in Coffeyville, Kansas, on September 3, 1970. It measured 17 1/2 inches around—about as big as a football! It weighed over a pound and a half.

# New Ways to Predict Wacky Weather

We now have all sorts of scientific equipment for studying and tracking weather, including laser telescopes, radar, satellites, and supercomputers. These tools help meteorologists forecast the weather more accurately so that people can be prepared when dangerous storms are going to hit areas where they live.

Even though we're better able to predict dangerous weather now than in the past, there's still no way to prevent it or change it. Forecasting isn't perfect either. So watch out and be prepared—wacky weather can show up anywhere without any warning!

# Glossary

**cumulonimbus**  a type of large cloud with a flat base and rounded edges, often piled high; also called a thunderhead

**eruption**  a sudden release of something (like lava or steam) that is under pressure

**hail**  pieces of ice that fall during a storm

**lava**  hot melted rock that flows from a volcano

**meteorologist**  a scientist who studies the atmosphere, weather, and climate

**rime ice**  a white frost formed when fog droplets touch objects in extremely cold temperatures

**stratosphere**  the part of the atmosphere that extends about 7 miles to 30 miles above the earth's surface

**stratovolcano**  a cone-shaped volcano

**updraft**  an upward movement of air

**visibility**  the distance at which objects can be seen clearly under certain weather conditions

**vortex**  whirling water or air that circles and drags things toward its center

**waterspout**  a funnel-shaped, cloud-filled, spinning column of wind attached to the base of a cloud over water